CULTURE, SOCIETY & GLOBALIZATION
World Connections Series

Written by Erika Gasper

GRADES 5 - 8
Reading Levels 3 - 4

Classroom Complete Press

P.O. Box 19729
San Diego, CA 92159
Tel: 1-800-663-3609 / Fax: 1-800-663-3608
Email: service@classroomcompletepress.com

www.classroomcompletepress.com

ISBN-13: 978-1-55319-480-4

© 2010

Critical Thinking Skills

Culture, Society & Globalization

Skills for Critical Thinking	Reading								Hands-on Activities
	Section 1	Section 2	Section 3	Section 4	Section 5	Section 6	Section 7	Section 8	
LEVEL 1 Remembering									
• List Details/Facts	✓	✓	✓	✓	✓	✓	✓	✓	
• Recall Information	✓	✓	✓	✓	✓	✓	✓	✓	✓
• Match Vocabulary to Definitions					✓	✓		✓	
• Define Vocabulary	✓	✓	✓	✓	✓	✓	✓	✓	
• Sequence	✓			✓					✓
LEVEL 2 Understanding									
• Demonstrate Understanding	✓	✓	✓	✓	✓	✓	✓	✓	✓
• Describe	✓	✓	✓	✓	✓	✓	✓	✓	✓
• Classify		✓	✓	✓	✓	✓		✓	
LEVEL 3 Applying									
• Application to Own Life		✓	✓	✓	✓	✓	✓	✓	✓
• Organize and Classify Facts		✓	✓	✓	✓	✓	✓	✓	✓
• Infer Outcomes	✓	✓	✓	✓	✓	✓	✓	✓	✓
• Utilize Alternative Research Tools	✓	✓	✓	✓	✓	✓	✓	✓	✓
LEVEL 4 Analysing									
• Distinguish Meanings		✓	✓	✓	✓	✓	✓	✓	✓
• Make Inferences	✓	✓	✓	✓	✓	✓	✓	✓	✓
• Draw Conclusions	✓	✓	✓	✓	✓	✓	✓	✓	✓
• Identify Cause and Effect	✓	✓	✓	✓	✓	✓	✓	✓	✓
• Identify Supporting Evidence		✓		✓	✓	✓	✓	✓	✓
LEVEL 5 Evaluating									
• State and Defend an Opinion		✓	✓	✓	✓	✓	✓	✓	✓
• Make Recommendations		✓	✓	✓	✓	✓	✓	✓	✓
• Influence Community			✓	✓	✓	✓	✓	✓	✓
LEVEL 6 Creating									
• Compile Research Information	✓	✓	✓	✓	✓	✓	✓	✓	✓
• Design and Application	✓	✓		✓	✓				✓
• Create and Construct	✓	✓	✓	✓				✓	✓
• Imagine Alternatives		✓		✓	✓	✓	✓	✓	✓

Based on Bloom's Taxonomy

Contents

• • • • • • • • • • • • • • • • •

🍎 TEACHER GUIDE

✏️ STUDENT HANDOUTS

READING COMPREHENSION

EZ✓ EASY MARKING™ ANSWER KEY

OVERHEAD TRANSPARENCIES

✔ **6 BONUS Activity Pages!** Additional worksheets for your students
✔ **6 BONUS Overhead Transparencies!** For use with your projection system
or interactive whiteboard

FREE!

• Go to our website: **www.classroomcompletepress.com/bonus**
• Enter item CC5782
• Enter pass code CC5782D for Activity Pages. CC5782A for Overheads.

Assessment Rubric

· · · · · · · · · · · · · · · · · · · ·

Culture, Society & Globalization

Student's Name: _____ Assignment: _____ Level: _____

	Level 1	Level 2	Level 3	Level 4
Comprehension of the causes and effects of globalization	Demonstrates a limited understanding of the causes and effects of globalization; requires teacher intervention.	Demonstrates a basic understanding of the causes and effects of globalization; requires some intervention.	Demonstrates a good understanding of the causes and effects of globalization; requires no intervention.	Demonstrates an excellent understanding of the causes and effects of globalization; requires no intervention.
Responses to the text	Expresses responses to the text with limited effectiveness; inconsistently supported by proof from the text.	Expresses responses to the text with some effectiveness; supported by some proof from the text.	Expresses satisfactory responses to the text with some effectiveness; supported by satisfactory proof from the text.	Expresses thorough responses to the text with some effectiveness; thoroughly supported by proof from the text.
Analysis of key concepts related to globalization	Interprets various concepts from the text with limited, unrelated details and incorrect analysis.	Interprets various concepts from the text with some details but also some incorrect analysis.	Interprets various concepts from the text with satisfactory details and good analysis.	Interprets various concepts from the text with excellent details and thorough analysis.
Application of key concepts related to globalization	Demonstrates a limited ability to apply various concepts from the text to activities, discussions, and novel situations.	Demonstrates a basic ability to apply various concepts from the text to activities, discussions, and novel situations.	Demonstrates a satisfactory ability to apply various concepts from the text to activities, discussions, and novel situations.	Demonstrates a strong ability to apply various concepts from the text to activities, discussions, and novel situations.

STRENGTHS:

WEAKNESSES:

NEXT STEPS:

Teacher Guide

Our resource has been created for ease of use by both **TEACHERS** *and* **STUDENTS** *alike.*

Introduction

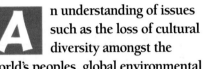

An understanding of issues such as the loss of cultural diversity amongst the world's peoples, global environmental problems, protecting human rights, and global health issues can be deepened through an understanding of globalization. Issues such as these can be examined through a study of the following themes: *the history of globalization, globalization in modern times, international languages, cultural homogenization, globalism and tourism, globalism and health, the global environment* and *international human rights law.* Students need to acquire an understanding of globalization in order to make informed decisions about civil matters and lifestyle choices that affect themselves, their families, and people around the world, and to understand different perspectives in debates about issues surrounding globalization.

How Is Our Resource Organized?

STUDENT HANDOUTS

Reading passages and **activities** (*in the form of reproducible worksheets*) make up the majority of our resource. The reading passages present important grade-appropriate information and concepts related to the topic. Embedded in each passage are one or more questions that ensure students understand what they have read.

For each reading passage there are **BEFORE YOU READ** activities and **AFTER YOU READ** activities.

- The BEFORE YOU READ activities prepare students for reading by setting a purpose for reading. They stimulate background knowledge and experience, and guide students to make connections between what they know and what they will learn. Important concepts and vocabulary from the chapters are also presented.
- The AFTER YOU READ activities check students' comprehension of the concepts presented in the reading passage and extend their learning. Students are

asked to give thoughtful consideration of the reading passage through creative and evaluative short-answer questions, research, and extension activities.

Writing Tasks are included to further develop students' thinking skills and understanding of the concepts. The **Assessment Rubric** (*page 4*) is a useful tool for evaluating students' responses to many of the activities in our resource. The **Comprehension Quiz** (*page 48*) can be used for either a follow-up review or assessment at the completion of the unit.

PICTURE CUES

This resource contains three main types of pages, each with a different purpose and use. A **Picture Cue** at the top of each page shows, at a glance, what the page is for.

 Teacher Guide
- Information and tools for the teacher

 Student Handouts
- Reproducible task sheets and drill sheets

 Easy Marking™ Answer Key
- Answers for student activities

EASY MARKING™ ANSWER KEY

Marking students' worksheets is fast and easy with our **Answer Key**. Answers are listed in columns – just line up the column with its corresponding worksheet, as shown, and see how every question matches up with its answer!

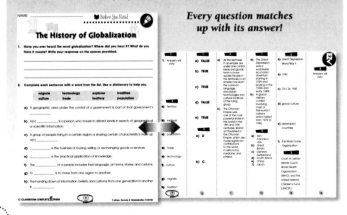

Every question matches up with its answer!

Bloom's Taxonomy

Our resource is an effective tool for any SOCIAL STUDIES PROGRAM.

Bloom's Taxonomy* for Reading Comprehension

The activities in this resource engage and build the full range of thinking skills that are essential for students' reading comprehension. Based on the six levels of thinking in Bloom's Taxonomy, assignments are given that challenge students to not only recall what they have read, but move beyond this to understand the text through higher-order thinking. By using higher-order skills of applying, analyzing, evaluating and creating, students become active readers, drawing more meaning from the text, and applying and extending their learning in more sophisticated ways.

Our resource, therefore, is an effective tool for any Social Studies program. Whether it is used in whole or in part, or adapted to meet individual student needs, this resource provides teachers with the important questions to ask, interesting content, which promote creative and meaningful learning.

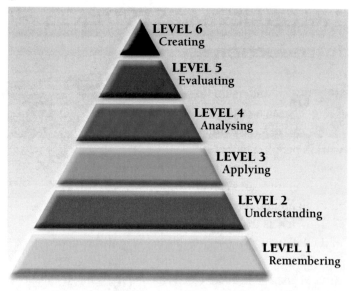

LEVEL 6 Creating
LEVEL 5 Evaluating
LEVEL 4 Analysing
LEVEL 3 Applying
LEVEL 2 Understanding
LEVEL 1 Remembering

BLOOM'S TAXONOMY: 6 LEVELS OF THINKING

Bloom's Taxonomy is a widely used tool by educators for classifying learning objectives, and is based on the work of Benjamin Bloom.

Vocabulary

chronic	human rights	quarantine
Colonial Empires	indigenous	resources
commons	infectious	Silk Road
cultural homogenization	international	territories
empire	mainstream	tourism
environment	migrate	treaty
epidemic	mother language	United Nations (UN)
global culture	official language	World Court
global warming	Ottoman Empire	World Trade
globalization	pandemic	Organization (WTO)

NAME: _____

The History of Globalization

1. **Have you ever heard the word globalization? Where did you hear it? What do you think it means? Write your response on the spaces provided.**

_____

_____

_____

2. **Complete each sentence with a word from the list. Use a dictionary to help you.**

migrate	technology	explorer	tradition
culture	trade	territory	population

a) A geographic area under the control of a government is part of that government's

_____.

b) A(n) _____ is a person who travels to distant lands in search of geographical or scientific information.

c) A group of people living in a certain region or sharing certain characteristics make up a(n) _____.

d) _____ is the business of buying, selling, or exchanging goods or services.

e) _____ is the practical application of knowledge.

f) The _____ of a people includes their language, art forms, stories, and customs.

g) To _____ is to move from one region to another.

h) The handing down of information, beliefs, and customs from one generation to another is _____.

The History of Globalization

When people use the word **globalization** today, they are usually describing how different nations around the world are sharing more goods, ideas, culture, systems of government, and even people as they move or **migrate** from place to place. The history of globalization begins with human migration from our origins in Africa to all other parts of the world. By about 40,000 years ago, humans occupied most of Europe, Asia, and Australia. By 15,000-20,000 years ago, humans also occupied most of North and South America.

What is globalization?

_____

_____

Historical Trade Routes

When people moved, they brought culture and technology with them. It was natural for people to trade goods and ideas with neighboring groups. As technology and governments developed, larger routes of trade became possible. A series of trade routes known as the **Silk Road** crisscrossed Eurasia, Asia, and the Middle East beginning in the first millenium B.C.E. After

Silk Road

Italian explorer Marco Polo returned from Asia with silk and jewels in 1295 C.E., Europeans began trading along the Silk Road as well. People traded not only goods along the Silk Road, but ideas as well. Many important scientific ideas and technologies migrated from Asia to Europe, including the magnetic compass, the printing press, and mathematics. Musical instruments and ideas migrated between many regions of the Silk Road. Traders brought cymbals from India to China and Europe. Early Persian reed instruments gave Europeans ideas that led to the invention of modern reed instruments such as the clarinet and oboe.

The History of Globalization

Empires and Globalization

At certain times in history, one country or region takes political and ecomonic control over other territories, forming an **empire**. Because all the **territories** or regions in an empire are under one control, ideas and goods tended to move quickly within the empire. For example, people in the territories of an empire may learn the common language of the ruling group. Older languages and ways of life are often lost in an empire. Technologies and cultural traditions from the ruling group spread to territories.

What is an empire?

_____

_____

Examples of Empires

The **Ottoman Empire** was one of the most powerful states in the world in the 15th and 16th centuries. It spanned from about 1300 C.E. to 1922, and at its height included most of southeastern Europe, Iraq, Syria, Israel, Egypt, much of North Africa, and most of the Arabian Peninsula. Islamic art and architecture flourished in the Ottoman Empire. Science and technology education was strong, and the Ottoman Empire made significant contributions to the world in such fields as astronomy, medicine, and physics.

The Ottoman Empire

In the 15th century, Portugal and Spain developed maritime technologies that enabled them to travel great distances on the ocean. This led to the expansion of the European Empires, or **Colonial Empires**. Britain, Spain, France, Portugal, and the Netherlands had extensive territories in North and South America, Africa, and the East Indies. Europeans colonized these lands, bringing their languages, technologies, and culture. Often, the Europeans clashed with native or indigenous populations, who struggled to preserve their own culture and languages as their way of life changed dramatically. Europeans also brought Africans to many colonies as slaves, who also struggled to keep their own cultural traditions alive. The mixing of these different populations influenced the modern societies that these former colonies would become.

After You Read 📖 NAME: _____

The History of Globalization

1. **Circle** the word **TRUE** if the statement is TRUE or **Circle** the word **FALSE** if it is FALSE.

   a) The Ottoman Empire was one of the most powerful states in the world in the 19th century.

   TRUE **FALSE**

   b) Musical instruments and ideas were traded on the Silk Road.

   TRUE **FALSE**

   c) The Colonial Empire included the territories of Britain, Spain, France, Portugal, and the Netherlands.

   TRUE **FALSE**

   d) Europe began trading along the Silk Road in the first millenium B.C.E.

   TRUE **FALSE**

   e) Humans occupied most of Europe, Asia, and Australia by about 40,000 years ago.

   TRUE **FALSE**

2. **Put a check mark (✓) next to the answer that is most correct.**

   a) Which region was *not* part of the Silk Road?

   ⃝ **A** Asia
   ⃝ **B** the Middle East
   ⃝ **C** Europe
   ⃝ **D** South Africa

   b) During what time period did the Colonial Empire expand rapidly as a result of the development of maritime technologies?

   ⃝ **A** first millennium B.C.E.
   ⃝ **B** 13th century C.E.
   ⃝ **C** 15th century C.E.
   ⃝ **D** 19th century C.E.

The History of Globalization

3. Answer each question with complete sentences.

a) Explain why older customs and traditions of groups of people are often lost in an empire.

_____

_____

_____

b) Describe the influence of the Ottoman Empire on the greater world.

_____

_____

_____

Research

4. How did important inventions, innovations, and ideas travel on the Silk Road?

Working as a class, divide a map of the Silk Road into geographical regions. Break into smaller groups and assign each group to research a region. Using the library or internet resources, research the history, culture, science, and technology of your region during the period of the Silk Road. Find out what objects and ideas originated in your region, and how those were carried to other regions along the Silk Road. Find out what objects or ideas were taken into your region from the Silk Road. Prepare a list of these exports and imports, and add this list to the Silk Road map.

Take turns sharing information by group until all of the areas on the map have been covered. As a class, try to trace the movement of new inventions and ideas along the Silk Road.

NAME: _____

Globalization in Modern Times

1. a) On the spaces provided, briefly describe the **Great Depression**.

_____

_____

_____

b) On the spaces provided, briefly describe **World War II**.

_____

_____

_____

2. Fill in the map labels with locations from the list below.

Great Britain	**Japan**	**China**
San Francisco, USA	**Geneva, Switzerland**	**South Africa**

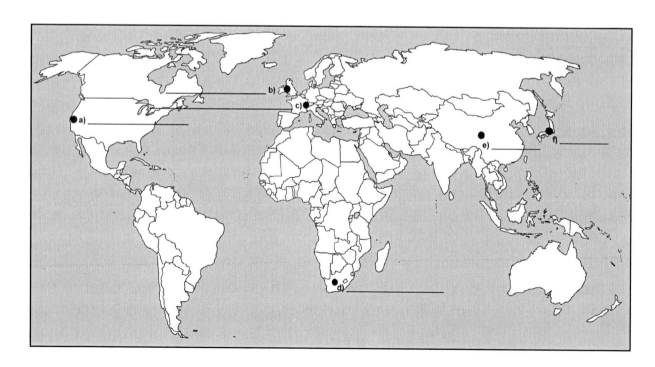

Globalization in Modern Times

From the 1920s through the 1940s, the world struggled through the Great Depression and then World War II. Nations directed their wealth, technology, and workforce to support war efforts. People around the world suffered, and it seemed as if the global system was going through a period of breakdown. After the end of World War II, leaders worked hard to form **international** agreements and organizations that would support economic and political interdependence between nations. Their hope was that a world that was tied together through trade and world governmental organizations that protected and supported human rights would be less likely to suffer through world wars in the future. The foundations for this renewed globalization that began right after World War II continued to be built upon through the second half of the 20th century.

How did leaders support globalization after World War II?

_____

_____

The United Nations

In 1945, representatives of 50 countries met in San Francisco at the United Nations Conference on International Organization. Together they wrote and signed the United Nations Charter with the goals of helping nations cooperate on issues such as international law, economic development, world peace, and human rights. On October 24, 1945, the **United Nations (UN)** officially came into being when a majority of signatories ratified the charter. The UN now has

The UN Headquarters in Geneva

its headquarters in New York City and Geneva, Switzerland, and has 192 member states, which make up almost all the independent nation states in the world today. The UN is made up of many bodies and agencies, including the International Court of Justice, also known as the **World Court**, the World Health Organization (WHO), and the United Nations Children's Fund (UNICEF).

Globalization in Modern Times

Speeding Up Globalization

During the second half of the 20th century, international organizations gained strength, trade between nations increased, and technology allowed people around the world to communicate and travel more easily. These changes sped up the pace of globalization. A **global culture** emerged as ideas, music, art, movies, and other forms of popular culture spread quickly across distant nations and regions. For example, a young person growing up in the United States in the late 20th century might watch Japanese cartoons, listen to music from Great Britain and the Caribbean, eat Chinese food, and play the internationally appealing game of soccer, or *football*, all in a typical day. By the end of the 20th century, satellite television and the Internet provided millions of people with instant access to news, opinions, and popular culture from around the world.

What changes made globalization go faster in the second half of the 20th century?

_____

_____

Concerns About Globalization

As people became more aware of the increasingly fast pace of globalization, concern arose about some of the harmful aspects of globalization. Trade agreements made it easier for companies to move factories out of developed countries to poorer areas with fewer labor and environmental laws. Natural resources were being quickly bought up and removed from developing and underdeveloped countries to make products that were sold in the developed world. The culture and

WTO Protests

languages of **indigenous**, or native, peoples around the world were becoming threatened by the adoption of Western culture and languages. These and other concerns led to large protests of international meetings of international trade and economic organizations, such as the **World Trade Organization (WTO)**.

Globalization in Modern Times

1. Fill in each blank with the correct word or date from the reading.

a) From the 1920s through the 1940s, the world struggled through the _____ and then _____.

b) In _____, representatives of 50 countries met in San Francisco at the United Nations Conference on International Organization.

c) On _____, the United Nations (UN) officially came into being when a majority of signatories ratified the charter.

d) During the second half of the 20th century, a _____ emerged as ideas, music, art, movies, and other forms of popular culture spread quickly across distant nations and regions.

e) Trade agreements made it easier for companies to move factories out of _____ to poorer areas with fewer labor and environmental laws.

f) Concerns about the harmful effects of globalization led to large protests of international meetings of international trade and economic organizations, such as the _____.

2. List three agencies of the United Nations on the spaces provided:

_____

_____

_____

Globalization in Modern Times

3. **Answer each question with complete sentences.**

a) Explain why globalization accelerated in the second half of the 20th century.

_____

_____

_____

_____

b) Describe three harmful effects of globalization.

_____

_____

_____

_____

_____

Research

4. Debate the pros and cons of globalization in modern times. Choose a position on a topic related to globalization in the second half of the 20th century. Use the library or internet to research your topic and write an opinion paper defending your position.

Possible topics may include:

- Globalization helps/harms the economies of underdeveloped nations;
- People's lifestyles in developing nations are better/worse because of globalization;
- The trade of products between countries is good/bad for the people who make the products;
- Globalization helps/harms the environment.

Read and respond to your classmates' opinion papers.

NAME: _____

International Languages

1. On the spaces provided, list all the languages you speak, beginning with the first one you learned.

_____

_____

_____

2. On the spaces provided, list all the languages spoken by older members of your family, including aunts, uncles, grandparents, great-grandparents and previous generations.

_____

_____

_____

_____

_____

_____

_____

3. On the spaces provided, explain whether your family uses fewer languages, more languages, or about the same number of languages now than it has in the past. Explain any changes in the use of languages by your family over the generations.

_____

_____

_____

International Languages

With globalization comes the need to communicate across diverse parts of the world. In the days of the Colonial Empire, European languages such as English, French, and Spanish spread to the colonies and became official languages of government, business, and trade. Governments and trade organizations in other regions of the world also spread official languages, such as Mandarin Chinese. The United Nations conducts business in six **official languages**: Arabic, Chinese, English, French, Russian, and Spanish. Many children learn one or more of these international languages in schools in order to effectively communicate in the world. Mandarin Chinese is spoken by the greatest number of people in the world. French and English are among the most widely spoken languages geographically.

World Languages Integrated

What language is spoken by the greatest number of people in the world?

_____

Preservation of Mother Languages

As the spread of English and other international languages became common in the last century, languages spoken in smaller regions or by smaller groups were less likely to be handed down from generation to generation. Some languages have even gone extinct, with no speakers of the language alive today. International efforts have grown to preserve the world's languages, which number over 6,900! These languages are documented by the organization Ethnologue www.ethnologue.com. Languages learned at home, passed down through families and communities, are sometimes called **mother languages**. International Mother Languages Day is celebrated every year on February 21.

International Languages

1. **On the spaces provided, list the six official languages of the United Nations:**

   _____

   _____

   _____

   _____

   _____

   _____

2. **Fill in each blank with the correct word from the reading.**

   a) With globalization comes the need to _____ across diverse parts of the world.

   b) In the days of the Colonial Empire, _____ languages such as English, French, and Spanish spread to the colonies.

   c) Languages of government, business, and trade are sometimes called _____ languages.

   d) A person's first language is sometimes called a _____ language.

   e) Some languages have even gone _____ with no speakers of the language alive today.

International Languages

3. **a)** On the spaces provided, explain how globalization has led to the use of a few official languages worldwide.

_____

_____

_____

b) On the spaces provided, explain why it is important to preserve the mother languages of the world.

_____

_____

_____

Research

4. Find out more about your family's mother languages. Interview family members and use the library and internet resources to find out more about the languages spoken by previous generations of your family. You may wish to create a family tree with languages listed beneath each person. Choose one or more of your family's mother languages, and research the following:

- The historical roots of the language;
- The geographical areas in which the language was spoken;
- How to say basic greetings in the language;
- How many speakers of the languages still exist today.

Using this information, create a poster showcasing your language. Hold a celebration of International Mother Languages Day in your classroom (you do not need to wait until February 21). During the celebration, display the posters and learn how to greet one another in each of the languages.

Cultural Homogenization

1. **a)** Use a dictionary to look up the word HOMOGENEOUS. Write the definition on the spaces provided.

    The definition of **homogeneous** is:

    _____

    _____

    b) Based on the definition of homogeneous and your understanding of globalization, what do you think the term **cultural homogenization** means? Write your ideas on the spaces provided.

    _____

    _____

    _____

2. **Use the words in the box to answer each question. You may use a dictionary to help you.**

media	conservatory	indigenous	fad

    ☐ **a)** What is a place where musicians teach and learn music?

    ☐ **b)** What are movies, television, and the internet?

    ☐ **c)** What is a practice, interest, or product that is especially popular for a short period of time?

    ☐ **d)** What is another word for people who are native to a certain region?

Cultural Homogenization

European—or Western—culture spread to the United States and the other European colonies during the Colonial Empire. When globalization sped up after World War II, the United States was a dominant economic and political force in the world. This led to the continued spread of Western culture around the world. The process of one culture becoming dominant, or **mainstream**, in areas that previously had many different cultural traditions is sometimes called **cultural homogenization**.

STOP

What is cultural homogenization?

_____

_____

How does Western culture spread?

The languages and customs of Europeans began to spread around the world as people and goods moved between different nations of the European empires. By the 1900s, English had become a language learned around the world. Conservatories and ensembles in many areas of the world embraced Western

McDonalds Restaurant in Asia

music, instrumentation, and musical ideas. The development of media in the West, such as movies and then television and the internet, spread Western popular culture. People around the world saw Western movie and television stars, as well as the lifestyles and fads they portrayed on the screen. Demand for Western products grew, and the United States exported everything from clothing to cars to fast food. By the end of the 1900s, most Westernized products were made cheaply in other nations and consumed around the world. Huge American corporations, such as McDonalds and Wal-Mart, had outlets to sell products in hundreds of nations around the world.

Cultural Homogenization

Cultural Homogenization in the United States

Cultural homogenization has even happened within the United States. A hundred years ago, people did not travel as much from place to place. Before television, people sought entertainment at local theaters from local artists. Many products, such as clothing and furniture, were made in the home or by local merchants. Produce and meats were grown at home or by local farmers. Food was almost always prepared at home using recipes passed down in families or communities. As a result, many cultural differences existed from region to region within the United States. The lifestyle of a family living in New England looked and felt very different from those in Georgia or California, for example. But by the end of the 1900s, most Americans sought entertainment from internally known artists on national and international media outlets, and bought everyday products from clothes to prepared foods from national or international companies. National chain stores operated outlets in towns around the country. Regional differences declined.

During what time period did cultural homogenization affect the United States?

_____

_____

Protecting Cultural Diversity

Although cultural homogenization allows people from different regions and ethnic backgrounds to share a common language and world culture, people around the world have also become aware of the need to preserve traditional and indigenous cultural traditions. In the United States, organizations like the Library of Congress American Folklife Center work to preserve recordings and media documentation of cultural traditions from the diverse ethnic and regional groups that make up the United States. Internationally, August 9 is celebrated as Indigenous Peoples' Day, to mark the first meeting, in 1982, of a United Nations commission to protect the human rights and cultural traditions of the world's indigenous peoples. Local groups working for the protection and preservation of traditional and indigenous cultures exist now in nearly all parts of the world, yet passing down languages and

Native American Dream Catcher

cultural heritage is still challenging in the face of global cultural homogenization.

Cultural Homogenization

1. **Answer each question using the term or date from the reading.**

[_____]	**a)**	What is the process of one culture becoming dominant, or mainstream, in areas that previously had many different cultural traditions?
[_____]	**b)**	On what date is Indigenous People's Day celebrated?
[_____]	**c)**	What U.S. organization works to preserve recordings and media documentation of cultural traditions from the diverse ethnic and regional groups that make up the United States?
[_____]	**d)**	What culture spread around the world beginning with the Colonial Empire and continuing throughout the last century?

2. **On the spaces provided, list 10 businesses, products, or artists that you think would most likely be recognized by children your age living in another country.**

_____

_____

_____

_____

_____

_____

_____

_____

Cultural Homogenization

3. a) On the spaces provided, explain how Western culture spread to the rest of the world.

_____

_____

_____

b) On the spaces provided, describe some of the ways in which life in a small town in the United States would have been different a hundred years ago compared to today.

_____

_____

_____

_____

Research

4. How does cultural homogenization affect indigenous people? Choose a certain indigenous group of people in the United States or another part of the world. Use the library or internet to research how this group has been affected by cultural homogenization over the last hundred years. Find out about:

- The historical cultural traditions of the group;
- When your group first encountered Western culture;
- How Western culture influenced the group over the last hundred years;
- The lifestyle of the group today;
- Traditions or practices that have been lost due to cultural homogenization.

Using this information, write a report to the United Nations outlining the problems that cultural homogenization has caused your indigenous group. In your report, make recommendations as to how the group's traditional culture can be preserved and passed down to future generations.

Celebrate Indigenous People's Day in your classroom. Create posters displaying the cultural practices of your indigenous group, and display them at the celebration. Choose a panel to read the reports and make an overall bulleted list of recommendations that would help preserve the traditions of indigenous people around the world.

Globalism and Tourism

1. **Use the library or internet resources to find out more about the terms DEVELOPED, DEVELOPING, and UNDERDEVELOPED NATIONS. Then, use your own words to define these terms using the spaces provided.**

   A **developed nation** is:

   _____

   _____

   A **developing nation** is:

   _____

   _____

   An **underdeveloped nation** is:

   _____

   _____

2. **What do you think the term *tourism* means? How is tourism different from other kinds of travel? Write your response on the spaces provided. You may use a dictionary to help you.**

   _____

   _____

   _____

   _____

Globalism and Tourism

Travel for leisure, or **tourism**, was once a pastime available mainly to people who were very wealthy or members of a powerful ruling class. However, that changed dramatically during the course of the 1900s with the advent of airplanes and the growth of the air travel industry. The cost of international travel became affordable to many people. By the 1950s, 25 million people had traveled to a foreign country. In the year 2000, nearly 700 million people visited a foreign country.

What industry allowed the growth of international travel?

_____

_____

Benefits and Problems of Tourism

When travelers from wealthy, developed nations visit developing or underdeveloped nations, they bring money that can benefit the local economy. Visitors may take tours of local historical sites, view natural wildlife, eat local foods, or attend performances of local artists. These activities can help support local people. But travelers also bring traffic, congestion, garbage, and Western culture to an area. Natural and historical sites can be overwhelmed or even destroyed by travelers. Construction of hotels, restaurants, and roads to accommodate tourists can also have a negative ecological and cultural impact in a region.

Palm Trump Hotel in Dubai

Even the economic impact of tourism can have negative effects. Economies of developing and underdeveloped host countries may become dependent on tourism. But since tourism is a leisure activity, it decreases significantly during periods of economic downturn in developed nations, and then the economies of tourism-depended nations suffer greatly. Water, food, and other natural resources in host countries may be used more for tourists who can pay a higher price for them than for local indigenous people.

Globalism and Tourism

1. **Use the words in the box to answer each question.**

tourism	economy	congestion
dependent	resources	indigenous

[_____] **a)** What are air, water, and food?

[_____] **b)** What is the system of money and goods?

[_____] **c)** What are people who are native to a certain region called?

[_____] **d)** What is travel for fun or personal interest?

[_____] **e)** Which term means having to rely on something for support?

[_____] **f)** Which word describes an excessive amount of people in one place?

2. **Put a check mark (✓) next to the answer that is most correct.**

a) **How many people have traveled internationally by the 1950s?**

○ **A** 1 million
○ **B** 25 million
○ **C** 50 million
○ **D** 700 million

b) **How many people traveled internationally in the year 2000?**

○ **A** 1 million
○ **B** 25 million
○ **C** 50 million
○ **D** 700 million

Globalism and Tourism

3. a) On the spaces provided, explain what you think is the main benefit of hosting tourism for developing and underdeveloped nations. Defend your reasoning.

_____

_____

_____

_____

b) On the spaces provided, explain what you think is the main problem of hosting tourism for developing and underdeveloped nations. Defend your reasoning.

_____

_____

_____

_____

Research

4. How does tourism affect people in developing or underdeveloped regions? Choose a popular tourist destination in a developing or underdeveloped nation. Use the library or internet to research how indigenous or other local people have been affected by the tourist activities. Find out about:

- Why tourists visit the area and what activities they usually do there;
- Who are the indigenous groups in the area and other local people;
- How has the local economy been affected by tourist activity;
- Whether local people benefit from tourists;
- The environmental and social problems caused by tourism.

Using this information, write a report outlining the benefits and problems of tourism in your region. In your report, make recommendations about how to make tourism more beneficial to local people, and how to lessen, or help fix, any problems related to tourism.

Globalism and Health

1. Think for a moment about how a modern Western lifestyle affects people's health. For example, think about:

- inventions and technologies in medicine and in everyday life;
- the ways in which a Western lifestyle affects how active people are;
- the foods people eat in modern Western societies.

a) List three ways that a modern Western lifestyle might help people stay more healthy.

_____

_____

_____

b) List three ways that a modern Western lifestyle might harm people's health.

_____

_____

_____

2. Match the term on the left to its definition on the right. You may use a dictionary to help you.

1	diabetes	a chronic lung disease that inflames and narrows the airways	A
2	asthma	harmful materials that are put into the environment by people	B
3	obesity	a disease in which the body does not produce or properly use insulin, a hormone needed to process sugars	C
4	preservation	the process of handling food to keep it from spoiling	D
5	pollution	a medical condition in which excess body fat builds up to the point where it harms health	E

Globalism and Health

The spread of Western culture affects the health of people around the world. On the positive side, the spread of Western medical technologies, including vaccinations, medications, and surgical tools, has helped lessen the impact of many diseases and health problems. Even the spread of everyday tools and technologies, such as refrigeration for food preservation, has helped people around the world stay healthy. On the negative side, the spread of Western products from cigarettes to fast foods has harmed the health of many people around the world. The adoption of a Western diet puts people at risk for diabetes and obesity. The development of industry harms the quality of the air and water in a region, putting people at risk for pollution-related diseases, such as asthma and heart disease. Also, as a society becomes more developed, people become less active. People walk less and depend more on vehicles for transportation. Tasks that once involved physical labor, such as washing clothes, are more likely to be done by a machine. A less active lifestyle can lead to ongoing, or **chronic**, health problems.

STOP

What diseases are related to pollution?

_____

_____

The Spread of Infectious Diseases

Hundreds of millions of people travel from country to country around the world each year. This creates the possibility of the quick spread of **infectious** diseases, or diseases that spread from person to person by contact or through the air. A disease **epidemic** occurs when there are more cases of that disease than normal. A **pandemic** is a worldwide epidemic of a disease. Officials at the World Health Organization (WHO) monitor the spread of infectious diseases, such as influenza and smallpox, and issue alerts and advice to governments to help contain the spread of epidemics. During an epidemic or pandemic, people may be asked to wear face masks, avoid congregating at social events, such as musical performances, and to restrict travel to certain areas. Officials may also **quarantine** infected people, asking them to stay home or in separate areas of hospitals.

Students Protecting Themselves with Face Masks

Globalism and Health

1. **Write each term beside its meaning.**

disease	infectious	epidemic	pandemic
quarantine	chronic	refrigeration	WHO

[_____] **a)** an ongoing medical condition that lasts a long time

[_____] **b)** a condition that harms health

[_____] **c)** the practice of keeping foods at a low temperature to prevent spoiling

[_____] **d)** a disease that can be passed from person to person

[_____] **e)** the organization that monitors the spread of infectious diseases around the world

[_____] **f)** when there are more cases of that disease than normal

[_____] **g)** the practice of keeping infected people away from others to slow the spread of an infectious disease

[_____] **h)** a worldwide epidemic of a disease

2. **Circle the chronic health problems that can be caused by a Western lifestyle. Underline the infectious diseases.**

asthma   obesity   influenza

smallpox   heart disease

Globalism and Health

3. **a)** On the spaces provided, explain why people may be more likely to get certain chronic health problems because of globalization.

_____

_____

_____

_____

b) On the spaces provided, explain why the spread of infectious diseases may occur more quickly because of globalization, and describe ways in which people can help slow the spread of an infectious disease during a pandemic.

_____

_____

_____

_____

Research

4. How can you stay healthy in a globalized world? Use the library or internet to research how people in Westernized societies can avoid common chronic health problems and infectious diseases. Find out about:

- How to make healthy food choices;
- The amount of physical activity needed to stay healthy, and some ways to stay active;
- How to avoid pollution problems, and ways communities can work together to clean up a polluted environment;
- Ways to avoid catching or passing infectious diseases.

Using this information, create a poster to teach people ways to stay healthy in our society. Display the posters around your school to help inform others.

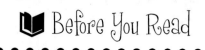 **Before You Read**

NAME: _____

The Global Environment

1. **a)** Use a dictionary to look up the word RESOURCE. Write the definition on the spaces provided.

The definition of **resource** is:

_____

_____

b) On the spaces provided, list 4 resources you need to survive and describe where you get those resources from.

_____   _____

_____   _____

_____   _____

_____   _____

2. Think about the air that surrounds Earth, or the atmosphere. Do you think that pollution put into the air by one country always stays above that country? Why or why not? Write your response on the spaces provided.

_____

_____

_____

 Reading Passage

The Global Environment

People and all other living things require **resources**, such as air, water, and food, from nature in order to survive. Living things must find these resources in their **environment**, or surroundings. Industrialization and population growth place demands on resources, and also cause pollution. These environmental problems have spread around the world with globalization. But the awareness of these problems and the science and technology needed to solve them has also spread, especially over the last few decades. People have become more aware that the world's people and all other living things share certain environmental **commons**, such as the oceans and the atmosphere.

STOP

What are resources?

_____

_____

International Treaties

As people have become aware of the global nature of environmental problems, leaders from different nations and organizations have come together to formulate international **treaties**, or agreements, that protect the environment. Two such world treaties that aim to reduce greenhouse gas emissions are the **Kyoto Protocol of 1997** and the **UN Climate Change Conference in Copenhagen of 2009**. These gases are mainly produced by burning fossil fuels. They trap heat in the atmosphere, which has resulted in an increase in average global temperatures, or **global warming**. Global warming

Burning Fossil Fuels

can cause problems around the world, such as a rise in sea level, stronger storms, drought, changes in agricultural productivity, and the spread of tropical diseases.

The United Nations Convention on the Law of the Sea, adopted in 1982, is a comprehensive treaty governing the world's oceans. It acknowledges that the open oceans beyond nations' coastlines belong to all people, and that we all must work together to protect the oceans by regulating fishing, mining, oil exploration, shipping, and other activities that remove resources or add pollution.

The Global Environment

1. Fill in each blank with the correct word or date from the reading.

a) People and all other living things require _____ such as air, water, and food, from nature in order to survive.

b) Living things must find resources in their _____.

c) Leaders from different nations and organizations come together to formulate international _____, or agreements, that protect the environment.

d) The _____ is a treaty which aims to reduce emissions of the greenhouse gases.

e) The _____, adopted in 1982, is a comprehensive treaty governing the world's oceans.

2. List five problems caused by global warming:

_____

_____

_____

_____

_____

The Global Environment

3. a) On the spaces provided, explain why environmental commons, such as the oceans and the atmosphere, must be protected by international treaties rather than by the laws of individual nations.

_____

_____

_____

_____

b) On the spaces provided, explain how the United Nations Convention on the Law of the Sea aims to protect the world's oceans.

_____

_____

_____

_____

Research

4. How does the Kyoto Protocol or UN Climate Change Conference in Copenhagen aim to reduce the effects of global warming? Use the library or internet to learn more about the Kyoto Protocol or Copenhagen Climate Change Conference. Find out about:

- Which nations drafted and signed the Kyoto Protocol or Copenhagen Climate Change Conference;
- The position of the United States on the Kyoto Protocol or Copenhagen Climate Change Conference;
- Which aspects of the Kyoto Protocol or Copenhagen Climate Change Conference received the most debate;
- The agreements made by developed nations under the Kyoto Protocol or Copenhagen Climate Change Conference;
- The agreements made by developing and underdeveloped nations under the Kyoto Protocol or Copenhagen Climate Change Conference.

Using this information, write a newspaper opinion piece about the Kyoto Protocol or Copenhagen Climate Change Conference. Provide readers with basic factual information about the treaty, and then give your opinions about its provisions. Discuss whether or not you think the treatment of different nations is fair, whether you think allowing carbon trading is a good idea, and whether or not you think the provisions of the Kyoto Protocol or Copenhagen Climate Change Conference go far enough to protect people all around the world from the effects of global warming.

NAME: _____

International Human Rights Law

1. a) Use the library or internet resources to find out more about the term HUMAN RIGHTS. Then, use your own words to define this term on the spaces provided.

Human rights means:

_____

_____

b) On the spaces provided, write 5 basic rights that you think all people around the world should have.

_____

_____

_____

_____

_____

2. Write each term beside its meaning. You may use a dictionary to help you.

discrimination	migrant	torture	genocide

[_____]	**a)**	the deliberate and systematic destruction of a racial, political, or cultural group
[_____]	**b)**	the act of applying prejudices, such as preferences for certain races, religions, or genders
[_____]	**c)**	a person who moves from one geographical location to another
[_____]	**d)**	the infliction of intense pain to punish or coerce

Reading Passage

International Human Rights Law

A fter World War II there was a growing movement to define and protect the **human rights** of all people on Earth, regardless of the nation in which they lived. In 1948, the United Nations passed the Universal Declaration of Human Rights, which for the first time in history outlined the basic civil, political, economic, social and cultural rights that all human beings should enjoy. This document served as a basis for developing international law that governs human rights.

STOP

What is the Universal Declaration of Human Rights?

_____

_____

International Treaties on Human Rights

A series of nine international treaties were passed as part of the international human rights law, which governs:

- the elimination of racial discrimination
- civil and political rights
- economic, social, and cultural rights
- the elimination of discrimination against women
- abolishing torture and other inhuman treatment
- the rights of the child
- the protection of migrant workers and their families
- the protection against enforced disappearance
- the rights of persons with disabilities

The World Court at the Hague

In addition to these nine treaties, many other agreements have been passed which add to international law governing topics such as the treatment of prisoners, the rights of indigenous peoples, the rights of older persons, and the elimination of hunger and malnutrition. All nations who are parties to the treaties agree to submit reports on the conditions and progress of human rights issues to the United Nations committee that deals with each treaty. The committee makes recommendations based on these reports and on any complaints about human rights abuses made by individuals or organizations that monitor human rights.

International human rights law also provides for the prosecution of war crimes, including genocide and torture. The most serious offenses are prosecuted by the International Criminal Court (ICC) at the Hague in the Netherlands. The United Nations may also set up Tribunals in areas affected by war and genocide to prosecute human rights abusers and seek justice for victims.

International Human Rights Law

1. Fill in each blank with the correct word or date from the reading.

a) After World War II there was a growing movement to define and protect the _____ of all people on Earth.

b) In 1948, the United Nations passed the _____, which for the first time in history outlined the basic rights that all human beings should enjoy.

c) This document served as a basis for developing _____ that governs human rights.

d) The most serious war crimes are prosecuted by the _____ at the Hague in the Netherlands.

e) The United Nations may also set up _____ in areas affected by war and genocide to prosecute human rights abusers and seek justice for victims.

2. On the spaces provided, list seven human rights issues that are covered by the treaties and agreements that make up international human rights law.

_____

_____

_____

_____

_____

_____

After You Read

International Human Rights Law

3. **a)** On the spaces provided, explain why it is important for human rights to be protected by international laws, rather than only by laws of individual nations.

_____

_____

_____

b) Are there any human rights not listed in the reading that you think should be protected by international law? Defend your position.

_____

_____

_____

Research

4. What are the goals of international human rights laws? Choose one of the international treaties or agreements that govern human rights. Suggestions are listed below:

- International Convention on the Elimination of All Forms of Racial Discrimination;
- International Covenant on Civil and Political Rights;
- International Covenant on Economic, Social and Cultural Rights;
- Convention on the Elimination of All Forms of Discrimination against Women;
- Convention against Torture and Other Cruel, Inhuman or Degrading Treatment or Punishment;
- Convention on the Rights of the Child;
- International Convention on the Protection of the Rights of All Migrant Workers and Members of Their Families;
- International Convention for the Protection of All Persons from Enforced Disappearance;
- Convention on the Rights of Persons with Disabilities.

Use the library or internet to research your treaty or agreement. Include its goals, how it is enforced, and any successes or problems it has had. Create a poster outlining the human rights that are protected by the treaty or agreement. Display the posters in your classroom.

Conduct a Mother Language Survey at your School

You learned about the spread of official languages and the loss of mother languages that can occur during globalization. You also learned about efforts to protect and preserve the world's mother languages. Find out more about the mother languages of the students at your school, whether they are being passed down to current generations, and inspire students to preserve their mother languages.

First, design a survey to find out information about mother languages of students at your school. Ask yourself the following questions:

- What format do you want the responses to be in? For example, you might consider short answers, lists, multiple choice, rankings. What format will be easiest to collect and analyze? What format will provide the most detailed information? Will you use different formats for different questions?
- How can you word questions to find out what languages are spoken at home, by whom, what languages were spoken by previous generations of students' families, and whether students themselves are able to speak all the mother languages of their families?
- Would you like to ask students to provide a couple of words or phrases in a mother language? Will you ask everyone for the same kind of phrase?
- How long should the survey take to complete?
- How many students will take the survey? If you do not survey every student at school, how can you get a sample of students that best represents the overall student population?
- How will you analyze the data you collect?
- How will you report the results?

Then, conduct and analyze your survey:

- Ask teachers for a few minutes of class time to introduce the survey. Hand out survey forms and request that students fill out and return the surveys as soon as possible, for example by the end of class time.
- Compile all of the students' responses and analyze the results. Compile a list of all mother languages, and how many students have family members that speak each language, and how many students are able to speak the mother languages. Analyze any other questions you asked.

Now, create a set of posters to display your results. You may want to create one poster that lists all of the mother languages in your family and the regions of the world where each language originates. Create another poster with the number results from all the questions in your survey. Create a third poster that celebrates mother languages and inspires students to learn mother languages. You may wish to include words from mother languages. Display your posters in a central area at your school so that students may view the results.

Conduct a United Nations Meeting

Conduct a meeting of the United Nations in your classroom about an important issue related to globalization, for example, health, the environment, the protection of indigenous peoples, or human rights.

First, use the library or internet resources to research how the United Nations and its subgroups conduct meetings on important issues, such as drafting treaties. If possible, watch news coverage of a United Nations meeting. Find out about:

- How nations are represented. Does each nation get one or more representatives? Who are they, for example, are they ambassadors or members of a national government?
- How are representatives of nations seated? Is there a system for ranking members according to how their nations are affected by the issue at hand?
- What is the protocol for allowing each representative to speak? In what order do they speak? Do they all get an equal amount of time? In what languages do they speak? How are speakers translated so that representatives from different nations can understand each other?
- What is the outcome of the meeting? For example, does the meeting result in a draft treaty, a list of recommendations, or some other product?

Then, work with your classmates to choose a topic of interest. You may wish to brainstorm a list and vote. Possible topics include:

- drafting a treaty to protect an environmental commons
- creating recommendations for the protection of mother languages
- creating recommendations to deal with epidemics and pandemics
- drafting additions to human rights law

Allow each student to select a nation to represent. Do some background research about each nation to determine how that nation would be affected by the chosen topic. Write a short speech outlining how the nation is affected, what position the nation takes on the issue, and what the nation would like to see in the treaty or recommendations.

Conduct the meeting. Allow each student to make his or her speech. Follow with a debate or discussion. Finally, create a draft of the final document.

Be a Conscious World Travel Agent

Plan international vacations for people that maximize the positive impacts and minimize the negative impacts of tourist activity on indigenous and local populations.

First, use the library and internet resources to research destinations that would be fun for tourists and beneficial for local peoples, cultures, and economies. Find out about:

- How different tourist activities impact local and indigenous people and local economies. Popular activities include visiting beaches, wildlife areas, and historical sites;
- How tourists can move from place to place with the least pollution or disruption to locals;
- What resources tourists will need, and where they can get these resources without affecting local people's ability to use the resources;
- How tourists' waste can be managed without polluting the local environment;
- How local and indigenous people can be supported by tourist activities, for example, by selling crafts or tickets to performances.

Then, plan a tour package. Include:

- Several destinations;
- How tourists will travel to different destinations on the tour;
- Where tourists will eat and sleep;
- What sites tourists will see and what activities they will participate in.

Finally, design a brochure to advertise your conscious travel tours. Your brochure should:

- Provide all necessary information about the tour package, including destinations, activities, and accommodations;
- Be interesting for people who want to travel internationally;
- Explain why your tours are more globally conscious, helping rather than harming local and indigenous people, their environment, and their economy.

Celebrate International Food Day

You learned how cultural homogenization has led to the adoption of Western customs, including diet, all around the world. You also learned how Western dietary fads like fast food can have a negative impact on people's health. Plan a potluck celebration with your class to celebrate international food day. You can promote awareness of healthy eating traditions from different cultures and encourage people to make healthy food choices.

First, have each student choose a culture represented in their family. Research the traditional diet of the culture, including:

- What staple crops were grown by the culture;
- How foods were traditionally prepared and cooked;
- What common dishes were served for breakfast, lunch, and dinner;
- How the cultural food traditions have been impacted by Western culture.

Have each student prepare a poster showing typical foods, crops, and cooking methods from their culture.

Then, have each student prepare a dish to share with the class during a potluck. Ask students to include a complete list of ingredients with their dishes so that students can be aware of any potential problems from food allergies.

During the potluck:

- Display all of the students' posters.
- Have each student introduce their dish, explaining where the dish originated, the ingredients, and the methods of preparation.
- Ask all students to try a taste of each dish that is within their personal dietary restrictions.
- Remind students to offer positive feedback.
- Ask students to share their opinions about their favorite dishes.

NAME: _____

Crossword Puzzle!

Across

1. the sharing of goods, ideas, culture, systems of government amongst people from different parts of the world

3. European formed _____ empires beginning in the 15th century

6. a global epidemic

8. a mother _____ is passed down from parents to children

10. native

11. an agreement between nations

14. a disease passed from person to person

Down

1. the increase in earth's average temperature

2. to move from one region or nation to another

4. Islamic art and architecture flourished in the _____ Empire

5. the spread of Western culture around the world has led to cultural _____

7. rights afforded to all people around the world by international law

9. things from nature that people and other living things need to survive

12. travel for leisure

13. a series of trade routes across Asia, the Middle East, North Africa, and Europe

Word List

colonial	human rights	migrate	Silk Road
global warming	indigenous	Ottoman	tourism
globalism	infectious	pandemic	treaty
homogenization	language	resources	

Word Search

Find all of the words in the Word Search. Words are written horizontally, vertically, diagonally, and some are even written backwards.

chronic	epidemic	indigenous	Ottoman	tourism
Colonial	global	infectious	pandemic	treaty
commons	global warming	international	quarantine	United Nations
culture	globalization	language	resources	World Court
empire	homogenization	mainstream	territory	WTO
environment	human rights	migrate		

```
G Q U A R A N T I N E Z I Q U A P W
H U I P E N V I R O N M E N T T V O
A T K L V A B J Y M S I R U O T W R
J H K B C C I M E D I P E A D H T L
C A P A N D E M I C O R C A B G A D
C H D F A L A N G U A G E D F L B C
R X R V G L O B A L I Z A T I O N O
A H E O M A E R T S N I A M L B E U
P O V F N W U Z I D T W R I K A G R
H M E H I I H T T Y E R E N S L D T
K O A F L J C A M I R Y S U N W L G
J G J D F C O M M O N S O H B A O A
G E B T R E A T Y O A U U E R R T Q
L N C O L O N I A L T E R I P M E S
O I D T W T W D O M I S C R Q I R U
P Z Y T T U D A W T O U E E A N R O
T A J O G S E Y J L N T S S T G I I
R T R M I G R A T E A B F L G H T T
H I H A P A S D F B L L I L A J O C
L O U N I T E D N A T I O N S C R E
I N D I G E N O U S J B H R U I Y F
E G H S T H G I R N A M U H F E P N
A S N F G M X C U L T U R E A I R I
```

After You Read 📖

Comprehension Quiz

25

Part A

(Circle) **TRUE** if the statement is TRUE or **FALSE** if it is FALSE.

1. Globalism began in the 20th century.
   TRUE   **FALSE**

2. The spread of Western culture has led to cultural homogenization.
   TRUE   **FALSE**

3. The rights of migrant workers are protected by international human rights law.
   TRUE   **FALSE**

4. The Kyoto Protocol or Copenhagen Climate Change Conference aims to protect and preserve the world's oceans.
   TRUE   **FALSE**

5. The International Criminal Court prosecutes serious war crimes.
   TRUE   **FALSE**

6. English is one of six official languages used by the United Nations.
   TRUE   **FALSE**

7. The Ottoman Empire included territories in North America, South America, and Australia.
   TRUE   **FALSE**

8. Infectious diseases spread from person to person.
   TRUE   **FALSE**

8

Part B

On the spaces provided, list five human rights that are protected by international law.

_____

_____

_____

_____

_____

5

48

SUBTOTAL: /13

Culture, Society & Globalization CC5782

 After You Read

Comprehension Quiz

Part C

Answer each question in complete sentences.

1. Explain the role of the Silk Road in historical globalization.   **4**

    _____

    _____

    _____

    _____

2. Describe two potential problems for indigenous people that are caused by globalization.   **2**

    _____

    _____

    _____

    _____

3. Describe two ways that globalization affects people's health.   **2**

    _____

    _____

    _____

    _____

4. Explain the role of international treaties in the protection of environmental commons.   **4**

    _____

    _____

    _____

    _____

SUBTOTAL: /12

3. Answers will vary.

1.

a) Great Depression, World War II

b) 1945

c) Oct. 24, 1945

d) global culture

e) developed countries

f) the World Trade Organization

2. Court of Justice (World Court), World Health Organization (WHO), and the United Nations Children's Fund (UNICEF)

1.

a) The Great Depression was a worldwide economic downturn starting in 1929 and ending in the 1930s and early 1940s.

b) A global military conflict involving most of the world's nations which lasted from 1939 to 1945.

2.

a) San Francisco, USA

b) Great Britain

c) Geneva, Switzerland

d) South Africa

e) China

f) Japan

3.

a) All the territories in an empire are under one control, ideas and goods tend to move quickly. People in the territories of an empire may learn the common language, and adopt technologies and cultural traditions of the ruling group.

b) The Ottoman Empire was one of the most powerful states in the world in the 15th and 16th centuries. Islamic art flourished in the Ottoman Empire, which also made significant contributions to the world in astronomy, medicine, and physics.

1.

a) FALSE

b) TRUE

c) TRUE

d) FALSE

e) TRUE

2.

a) D

b) C

---

1. Answers will vary.

1. Answers will vary.

2.

a) territory

b) explorer

c) population

d) trade

e) technology

f) culture

g) migrate

h) tradition

3.

a) The spread of Western culture began during the Colonial period and accelerated after WWII because the United States was a dominant political and cultural force in the world, and the development of media technology allowed for fast transmission of cultural ideas.

b) Answers will vary.

1.

a) cultural homogenization

b) August 9

c) Library of Congress American Folklife Center

d) Western

2.

Answers will vary.

1.

a) Homogeneous is something of the same or a similar kind or nature.

b) Answers will vary.

2.

a) conservatory

b) media

c) fad

d) indigenous

3.

a) Answers will vary, but should focus on the need to communicate for international trade, business, and governance.

b) Answers will vary, but should focus on the risk of extinction of languages spoken by small or remote groups of people.

1.

Arabic, Chinese, English, French, Russian, and Spanish.

2.

a) communicate

b) European

c) official

d) mother

e) extinct

1.

Answers will vary.

2.

Answers will vary.

3.

Answers will vary.

3.

a) Answers will vary but may include lack of physical activity, eating too much fast or processed food, pollution.

b) Answers will vary but may include people traveling more and carrying diseases from one place to another; slowing the spread of disease by avoiding places where people congregate, staying home while you are sick.

1.

a) chronic

b) disease

c) refrigeration

d) infectious

e) WHO

f) epidemic

g) quarantine

h) pandemic

2.

Asthma, obesity, and heart disease should be circled. Influenza and smallpox should be underlined.

1.

a) Answers will vary.

b) Answers will vary.

2.

1	C
2	A
3	E
4	D
5	B

3.

a) Answers will vary.

b) Answers will vary.

1.

a) resources

b) economy

c) indigenous

d) tourism

e) dependent

f) congestion

2.

a) B

b) D

1.

Answers will vary.

2.

Answers will vary.

3.
a) Answers will vary.

b) Answers will vary.

1.
a) human rights

b) Universal Declaration of Human Rights

c) international law

d) International Criminal Court

e) Tribunals

2. Answers may vary.

1.
a) Human rights are rights regarded as belonging fundamentally to all persons.

b) Answers will vary.

2.
a) genocide

b) discrimination

c) migrant

d) torture

3.
a) Answers will vary.

b) It acknowledges that the open oceans beyond nations' coastlines belong to all people, and that we all must work together to protect the oceans by regulating fishing, mining, oil exploration, shipping, and other activities that remove resources or add pollution.

1.
a) resources

b) environment

c) treaties

d) Kyoto Protocol or UN Climate Change Conference in Copenhagen

e) United Nations Convention on the Law of the Sea

2. A rise in sea level, stronger storms, drought, changes in agricultural productivity, and the spread of tropical diseases.

1.
a) A resource is something from nature that people need in order to stay alive.

b) Answers will vary.

2. Answers will vary.

Word Search Answers

Across

1. globalism
3. Colonial
6. pandemic
8. language
10. indigenous
11. treaty
14. infectious

Down

1. global warming
2. migrate
4. Ottoman
5. homogenization
7. human rights
9. resources
12. tourism
13. Silk Road

EZ✓

Part A

1. FALSE
2. TRUE
3. TRUE
4. FALSE
5. TRUE
6. TRUE
7. FALSE
8. TRUE

Part B

Answers will vary.

Part C

1. Ideas, inventions, goods, and people traveled from region to region across Asia, the Middle East, and North Africa on the Silk Road since the first millennium B.C. Europe later began trading on the Silk Road.

2. Answers will vary but may include loss of mother languages, reduction of environmental and cultural resources by tourism, poor health as a result of the adoption of Western diet and lifestyle.

3. Answers will vary but may include negative effects of Western fads like cigarette smoking and fast food, the quicker transmission of infectious diseases due to world trade, the spread of modern Western medical technology to many regions of the world.

4. Since all people depend on resources, such as the atmosphere and the oceans, they should be protected by international agreements. Since pollution from one area can travel quickly to other areas, efforts to stop pollution must be international.

Publication Listing

Ask Your Dealer About Our Complete Line

ENVIRONMENTAL STUDIES

ITEM #	TITLE
	MANAGING OUR WASTE SERIES
CC5764	Waste: At the Source
CC5765	Prevention, Recycling & Conservation
CC5766	Waste: The Global View
CC5767	Waste Management Big Book
	CLIMATE CHANGE SERIES
CC5769	Global Warming: Causes
CC5770	Global Warming: Effects
CC5771	Global Warming: Reduction
CC5772	Global Warming Big Book
	GLOBAL WATER SERIES
CC5773	Conservation: Fresh Water Resources
CC5774	Conservation: Ocean Water Resources
CC5775	Conservation: Waterway Habitats Resources
CC5776	Water Conservation Big Book
	CARBON FOOTPRINT SERIES
CC5778	Reducing Your Own Carbon Footprint
CC5779	Reducing Your School's Carbon Footprint
CC5780	Reducing Your Community's Carbon Footprint
CC5781	Carbon Footprint Big Book

LANGUAGE ARTS

ITEM #	TITLE
	WRITING SKILLS SERIES
CC1100	How to Write a Paragraph
CC1101	How to Write a Book Report
CC1102	How to Write an Essay
CC1103	Master Writing Big Book
	READING SKILLS SERIES
CC1116	Reading Comprehension
CC1117	Literary Devices
CC1118	Critical Thinking
CC1119	Master Reading Big Book

REGULAR & REMEDIAL EDUCATION

Reading Level 3-4 Grades 5-8

SCIENCE

ITEM #	TITLE
	ECOLOGY & THE ENVIRONMENT SERIES
CC4500	Ecosystems
CC4501	Classification & Adaptation
CC4502	Cells
CC4503	Ecology & The Environment Big Book
	MATTER & ENERGY SERIES
CC4504	Properties of Matter
CC4505	Atoms, Molecules & Elements
CC4506	Energy
CC4507	The Nature of Matter Big Book
	FORCE & MOTION SERIES
CC4508	Force
CC4509	Motion
CC4510	Simple Machines
CC4511	Force, Motion & Simple Machines Big Book
	SPACE & BEYOND SERIES
CC4512	Space - Solar Systems
CC4513	Space - Galaxies & The Universe
CC4514	Space - Travel & Technology
CC4515	Space Big Book
	HUMAN BODY SERIES
CC4516	Cells, Skeletal & Muscular Systems
CC4517	Nervous, Senses & Respiratory Systems
CC4518	Circulatory, Digestive & Reproductive Systems
CC4519	Human Body Big Book

SOCIAL STUDIES

ITEM #	TITLE
	NORTH AMERICAN GOVERNMENTS SERIES
CC5757	American Government
CC5758	Canadian Government
CC5759	Mexican Government
CC5760	Governments of North America Big Book
	WORLD GOVERNMENTS SERIES
CC5761	World Political Leaders
CC5762	World Electoral Processes
CC5763	Capitalism vs. Communism
CC5777	World Politics Big Book
	WORLD CONFLICT SERIES
CC5500	American Civil War
CC5511	American Revolutionary War
CC5512	American Wars Big Book
CC5501	World War I
CC5502	World War II
CC5503	World Wars I & II Big Book
CC5505	Korean War
CC5506	Vietnam War
CC5507	Korean & Vietnam Wars Big Book
CC5508	Persian Gulf War (1990-1991)
CC5509	Iraq War (2003-2010)
CC5510	Gulf Wars Big Book
	WORLD CONTINENTS SERIES
CC5750	North America
CC5751	South America
CC5768	The Americas Big Book
CC5752	Europe
CC5753	Africa
CC5754	Asia
CC5755	Australia
CC5756	Antarctica
	WORLD CONNECTIONS SERIES
CC5782	Culture, Society & Globalization
CC5783	Economy & Globalization
CC5784	Technology & Globalization
CC5785	Globalization Big Book
	MAPPING SKILLS SERIES
CC5786	Grades PK-2 Mapping Skills with Google Earth
CC5787	Grades 3-5 Mapping Skills with Google Earth
CC5788	Grades 6-8 Mapping Skills with Google Earth
CC5789	Grades PK-8 Mapping Skills with Google Earth Big Book

VISIT:

www.CLASSROOM COMPLETE PRESS.com

To view sample pages from each book

LITERATURE KITS™

ITEM #	TITLE
	GRADES 1-2
CC2100	Curious George (H. A. Rey)
CC2101	Paper Bag Princess (Robert N. Munsch)
CC2102	Stone Soup (Marcia Brown)
CC2103	The Very Hungry Caterpillar (Eric Carle)
CC2104	Where the Wild Things Are (Maurice Sendak)
	GRADES 3-4
CC2300	Babe: The Gallant Pig (Dick King-Smith)
CC2301	Because of Winn-Dixie (Kate DiCamillo)
CC2302	The Tale of Despereaux (Kate DiCamillo)
CC2303	James and the Giant Peach (Roald Dahl)
CC2304	Ramona Quimby, Age 8 (Beverly Cleary)
CC2305	The Mouse and the Motorcycle (Beverly Cleary)
CC2306	Charlotte's Web (E.B. White)
CC2307	Owls in the Family (Farley Mowat)
CC2308	Sarah, Plain and Tall (Patricia MacLachlan)
CC2309	Matilda (Roald Dahl)
CC2310	Charlie & The Chocolate Factory (Roald Dahl)
CC2311	Frindle (Andrew Clements)
CC2312	M.C. Higgins, the Great (Virginia Hamilton)
CC2313	The Family Under The Bridge (N.S. Carlson)
	GRADES 5-6
CC2500	Black Beauty (Anna Sewell)
CC2501	Bridge to Terabithia (Katherine Paterson)
CC2502	Bud, Not Buddy (Christopher Paul Curtis)
CC2503	The Egypt Game (Zilpha Keatley Snyder)
CC2504	The Great Gilly Hopkins (Katherine Paterson)
CC2505	Holes (Louis Sachar)
CC2506	Number the Stars (Lois Lowry)
CC2507	The Sign of the Beaver (E.G. Speare)
CC2508	The Whipping Boy (Sid Fleischman)
CC2509	Island of the Blue Dolphins (Scott O'Dell)
CC2510	Underground to Canada (Barbara Smucker)
CC2511	Loser (Jerry Spinelli)
CC2512	The Higher Power of Lucky (Susan Patron)
CC2513	Kira-Kira (Cynthia Kadohata)
CC2514	Dear Mr. Henshaw (Beverly Cleary)
CC2515	The Summer of the Swans (Betsy Byars)
CC2516	Shiloh (Phyllis Reynolds Naylor)
CC2517	A Single Shard (Linda Sue Park)
CC2518	Hoot (Carl Hiaasen)
CC2519	Hatchet (Gary Paulsen)
CC2520	The Giver (Lois Lowry)
CC2521	The Graveyard Book (Neil Gaiman)
	GRADES 7-8
CC2700	Cheaper by the Dozen (Frank B. Gilbreth)
CC2701	The Miracle Worker (William Gibson)
CC2702	The Red Pony (John Steinbeck)
CC2703	Treasure Island (Robert Louis Stevenson)
CC2704	Romeo & Juliet (William Shakespeare)
CC2705	Crispin: The Cross of Lead (Avi)

REGULAR EDUCATION

LANGUAGE ARTS

ITEM #	TITLE
	READING RESPONSE FORMS SERIES
CC1106	Reading Response Forms: Grades 1-2
CC1107	Reading Response Forms: Grades 3-4
CC1108	Reading Response Forms: Grades 5-6
CC1109	Reading Response Forms Big Book: Grades 1-6
	WORD FAMILIES SERIES
CC1110	Word Families - Short Vowels: Grades PK-1
CC1111	Word Families - Long Vowels: Grades PK-1
CC1112	Word Families - Vowels Big Book: Grades K-1
	SIGHT & PICTURE WORDS SERIES
CC1113	High Frequency Sight Words: Grades PK-1
CC1114	High Frequency Picture Words: Grades PK-1
CC1115	Sight & Picture Words Big Book Grades PK-1

INTERACTIVE WHITEBOARD SOFTWARE

ITEM #	TITLE
	CLIMATE CHANGE SERIES
CC7747	Global Warming: Causes Grades 3-8
CC7748	Global Warming: Effects Grades 3-8
CC7749	Global Warming: Reduction Grades 3-8
CC7750	Global Warming Big Box Grades 3-8
	HUMAN BODY SERIES
CC7549	Cells, Skeletal & Muscular Systems Grades 3-8
CC7550	Senses, Nervous & Respiratory Systems Grades 3-8
CC7551	Circulatory, Digestive & Reproductive Systems Grades 3-8
CC7552	Human Body Big Box Grades 3-8
	FORCE, MOTION & SIMPLE MACHINES SERIES
CC7553	Force Grades 3-8
CC7554	Motion Grades 3-8
CC7555	Simple Machines Grades 3-8
CC7556	Force, Motion & Simple Machines Big Box Grades 3-8
	WRITING SKILLS SERIES
CC7104	How to Write a Paragraph Grades 3-8
CC7105	How to Write a Book Report Grades 3-8
CC7106	How to Write an Essay Grades 3-8
CC7107	Master Writing Big Box Grades 3-8
	READING SKILLS SERIES
CC7108	Reading Comprehension Grades 3-8
CC7109	Literary Devices Grades 3-8
CC7110	Critical Thinking Grades 3-8
CC7111	Master Reading Big Box Grades 3-8
	SIGHT & PICTURE WORDS SERIES
CC7100	High Frequency Sight Words Grades PK-2
CC7101	High Frequency Picture Words Grades PK-2
CC7102	Sight & Picture Words Big Box Grades PK-2

MATHEMATICS

ITEM #	TITLE
	PRINCIPLES & STANDARDS OF MATH SERIES
CC3100	Grades PK-2 Number & Operations Task Sheets
CC3101	Grades PK-2 Algebra Task Sheets
CC3102	Grades PK-2 Geometry Task Sheets
CC3103	Grades PK-2 Measurement Task Sheets
CC3104	Grades PK-2 Data Analysis & Probability Task Sheets
CC3105	Grades PK-2 Five Strands of Math Big Book Task Sheets
CC3106	Grades 3-5 Number & Operations Task Sheets
CC3107	Grades 3-5 Algebra Task Sheets
CC3108	Grades 3-5 Geometry Task Sheets
CC3109	Grades 3-5 Measurement Task Sheets
CC3110	Grades 3-5 Data Analysis & Probability Task Sheets
CC3111	Grades 3-5 Five Strands of Math Big Book Task Sheets
CC3112	Grades 6-8 Number & Operations Task Sheets
CC3113	Grades 6-8 Algebra Task Sheets
CC3114	Grades 6-8 Geometry Task Sheets
CC3115	Grades 6-8 Measurement Task Sheets
CC3116	Grades 6-8 Data Analysis & Probability Task Sheets
CC3117	Grades 6-8 Five Strands of Math Big Book Task Sheets
	PRINCIPLES & STANDARDS OF MATH SERIES
CC3200	Grades PK-2 Number & Operations Drill Sheets
CC3201	Grades PK-2 Algebra Drill Sheets
CC3202	Grades PK-2 Geometry Drill Sheets
CC3203	Grades PK-2 Measurement Drill Sheets
CC3204	Grades PK-2 Data Analysis & Probability Drill Sheets
CC3205	Grades PK-2 Five Strands of Math Big Book Drill Sheets
CC3206	Grades 3-5 Number & Operations Drill Sheets
CC3207	Grades 3-5 Algebra Drill Sheets
CC3208	Grades 3-5 Geometry Drill Sheets
CC3209	Grades 3-5 Measurement Drill Sheets
CC3210	Grades 3-5 Data Analysis & Probability Drill Sheets
CC3211	Grades 3-5 Five Strands of Math Big Book Drill Sheets
CC3212	Grades 6-8 Number & Operations Drill Sheets
CC3213	Grades 6-8 Algebra Drill Sheets
CC3214	Grades 6-8 Geometry Drill Sheets
CC3215	Grades 6-8 Measurement Drill Sheets
CC3216	Grades 6-8 Data Analysis & Probability Drill Sheets
CC3217	Grades 6-8 Five Strands of Math Big Book Drill Sheets
	PRINCIPLES & STANDARDS OF MATH SERIES
CC3300	Grades PK-2 Number & Operations Task & Drill Sheets
CC3301	Grades PK-2 Algebra Task & Drill Sheets
CC3302	Grades PK-2 Geometry Task & Drill Sheets
CC3303	Grades PK-2 Measurement Task & Drill Sheets
CC3304	Grades PK-2 Data Analysis & Probability Task & Drill
CC3306	Grades 3-5 Number & Operations Task & Drill Sheets
CC3307	Grades 3-5 Algebra Task & Drill Sheets
CC3308	Grades 3-5 Geometry Task & Drill Sheets
CC3309	Grades 3-5 Measurement Task & Drill Sheets
CC3310	Grades 3-5 Data Analysis & Probability Task & Drill
CC3312	Grades 6-8 Number & Operations Task & Drill Sheets
CC3313	Grades 6-8 Algebra Task & Drill Sheets
CC3314	Grades 6-8 Geometry Task & Drill Sheets
CC3315	Grades 6-8 Measurement Task & Drill Sheets
CC3316	Grades 6-8 Data Analysis & Probability Task & Drill